How To Draw Flowers

A Step by Step Guide

Copyright © 2020 by SketchPert Press

Printed in the United States of America

9798673306161

INSTRUCTIONS

Here you will find the basic steps necessary to replicate the images found throughout this book.

Every flower starts out with a basic outline.

The second step fleshes out the outline a little more by more lines to its overall shape.

In the third step we begin adding the first details of the flower.

In the fourth step we add more details and some of the shading.

Once we get to the fifth step, we add the last details which give the flower its completed look.

The sixth step gives us a look at the final version of the flower with its full shading.

GRAPHING PAPER

Opposite each guide you will find a blank sheet of of 4x4 graph paper. By focusing in on the grids you can better pinpoint and emulate the art featured in the guides.

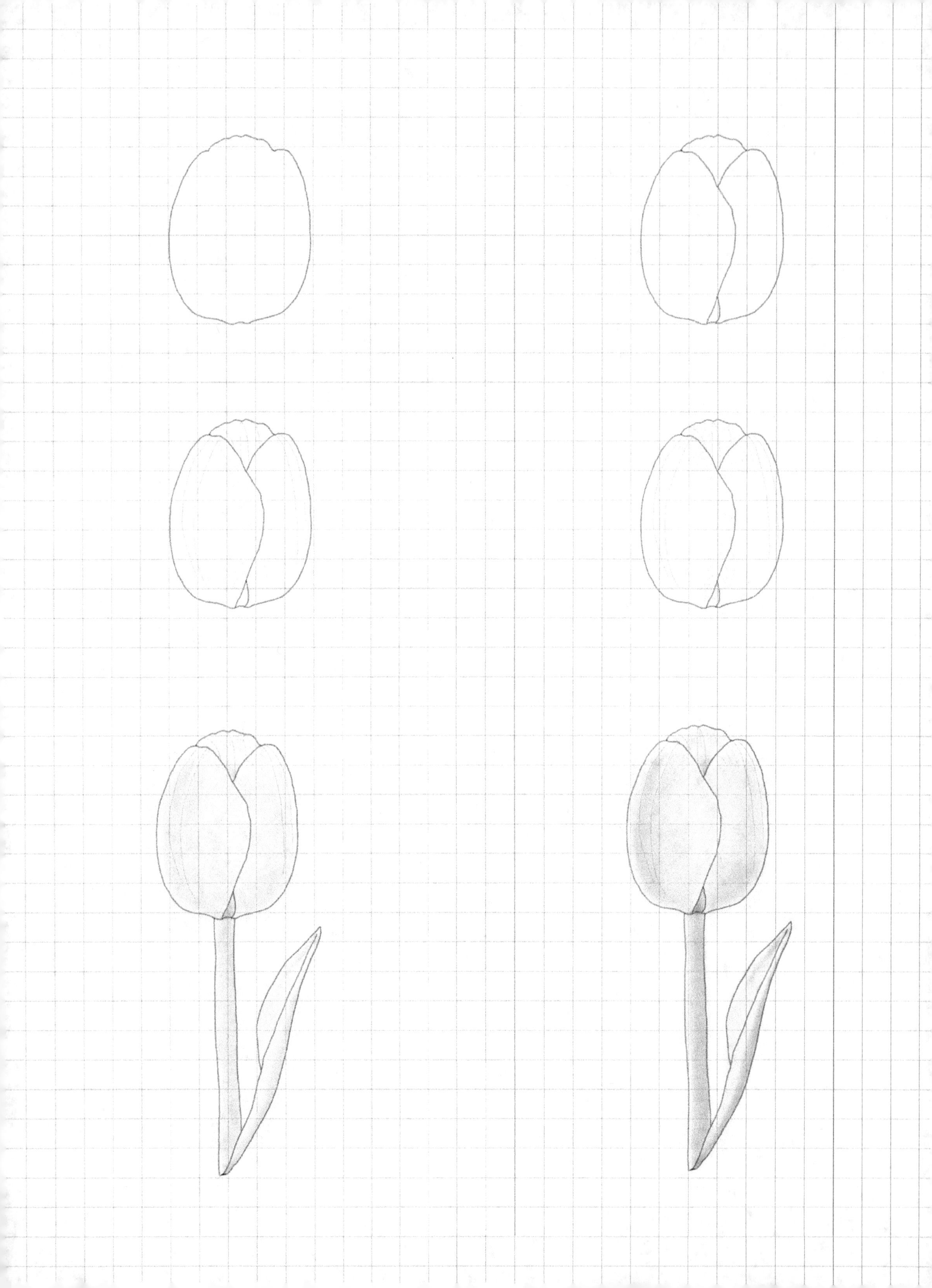

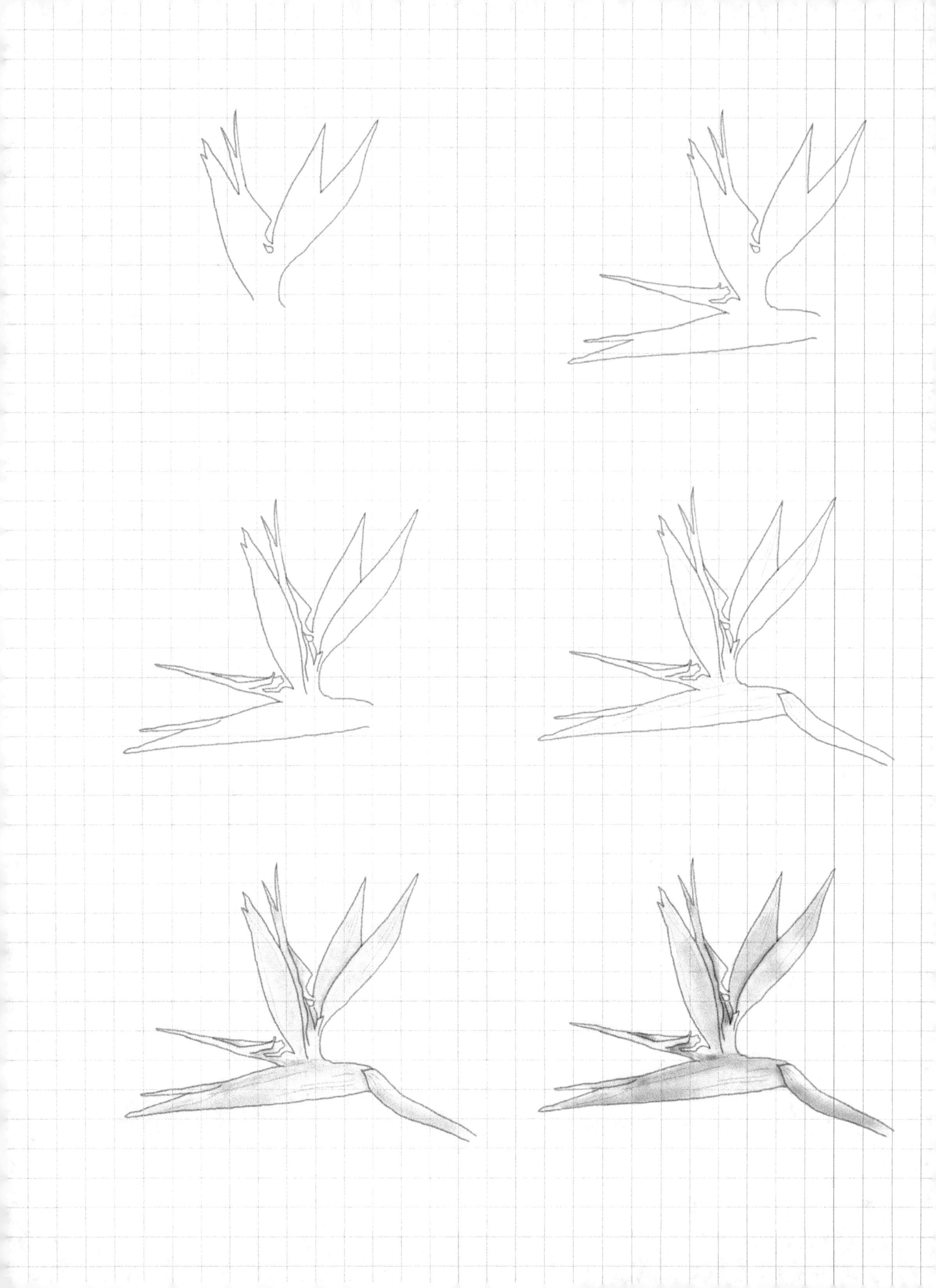

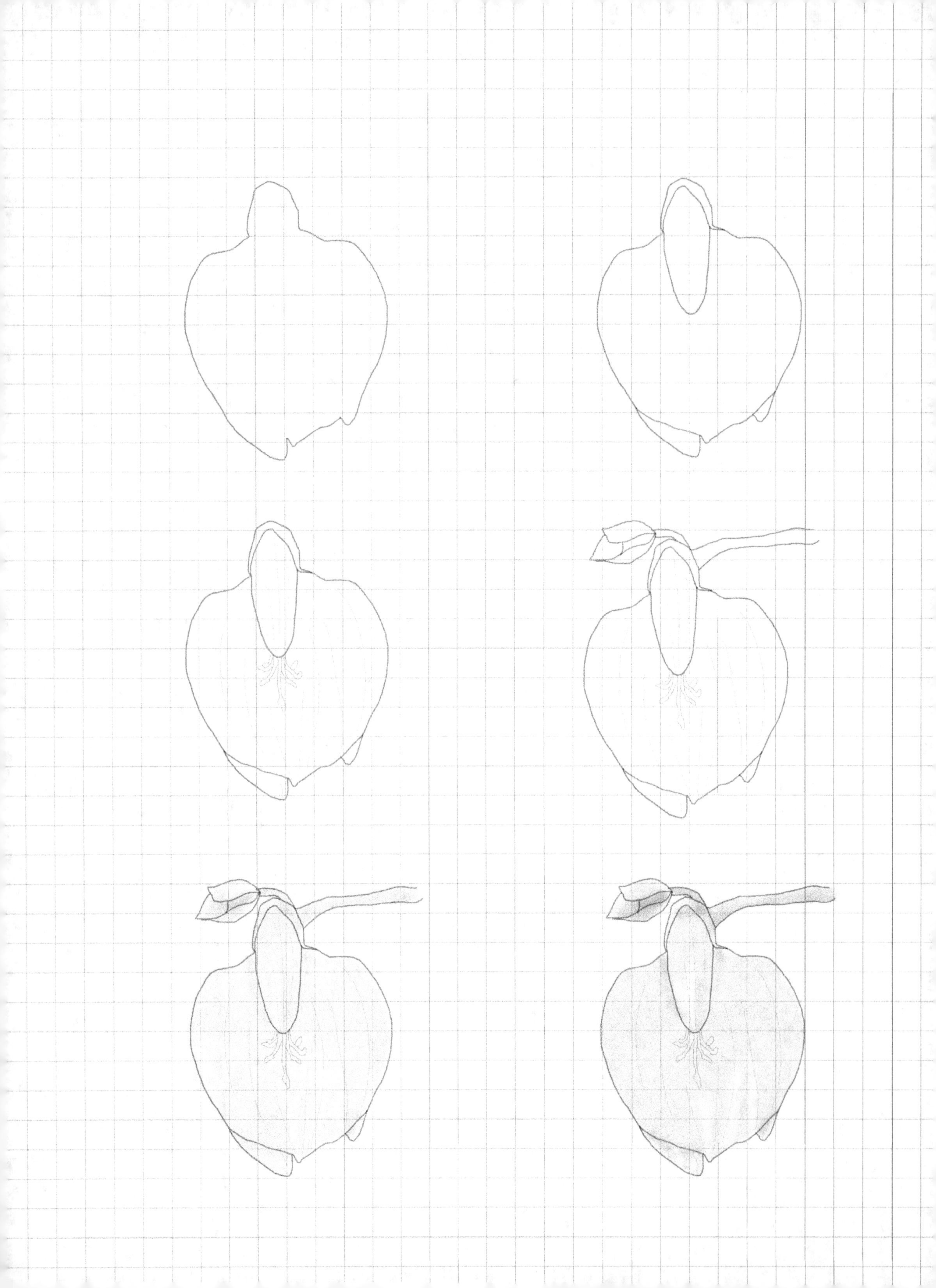

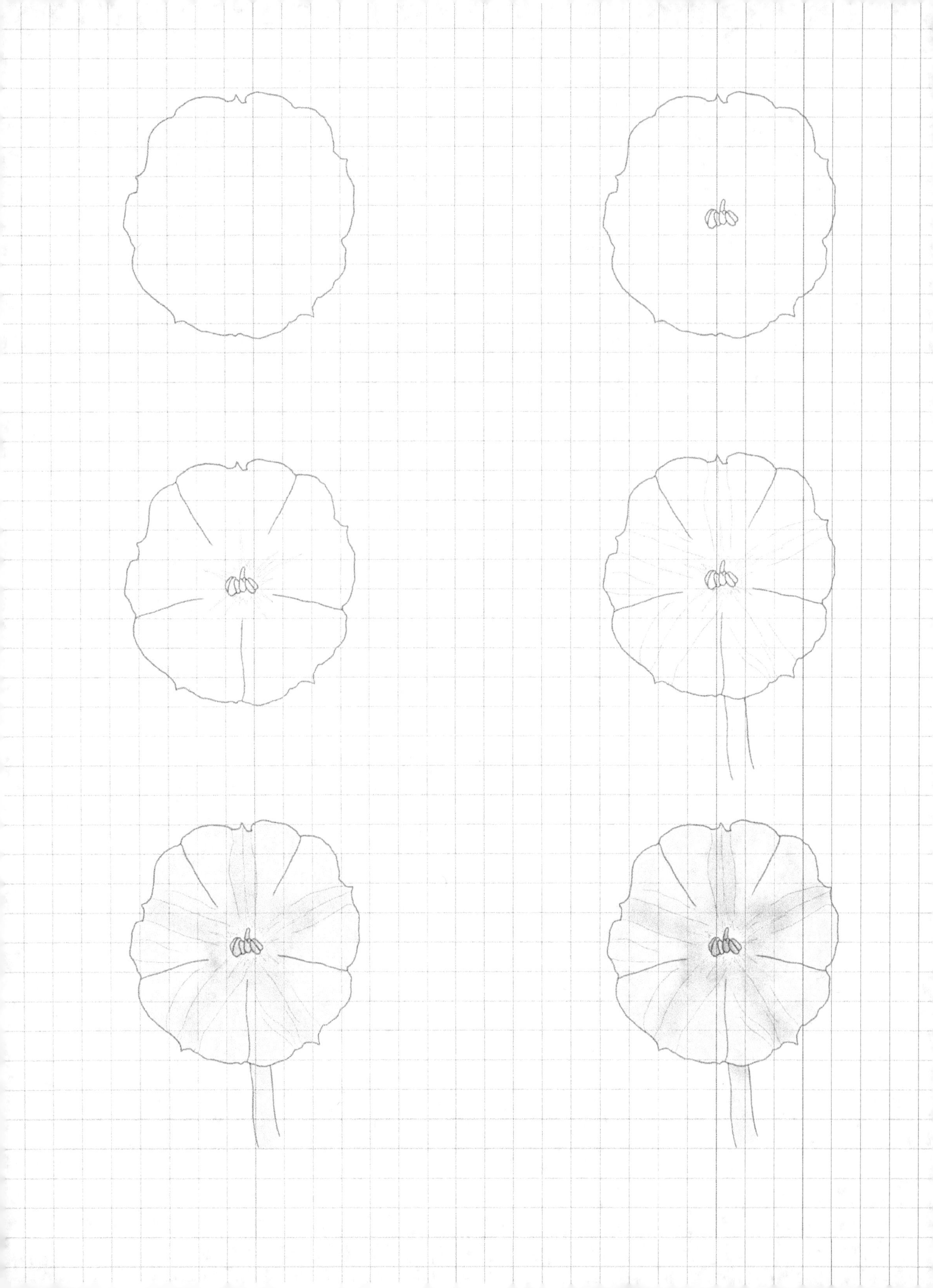

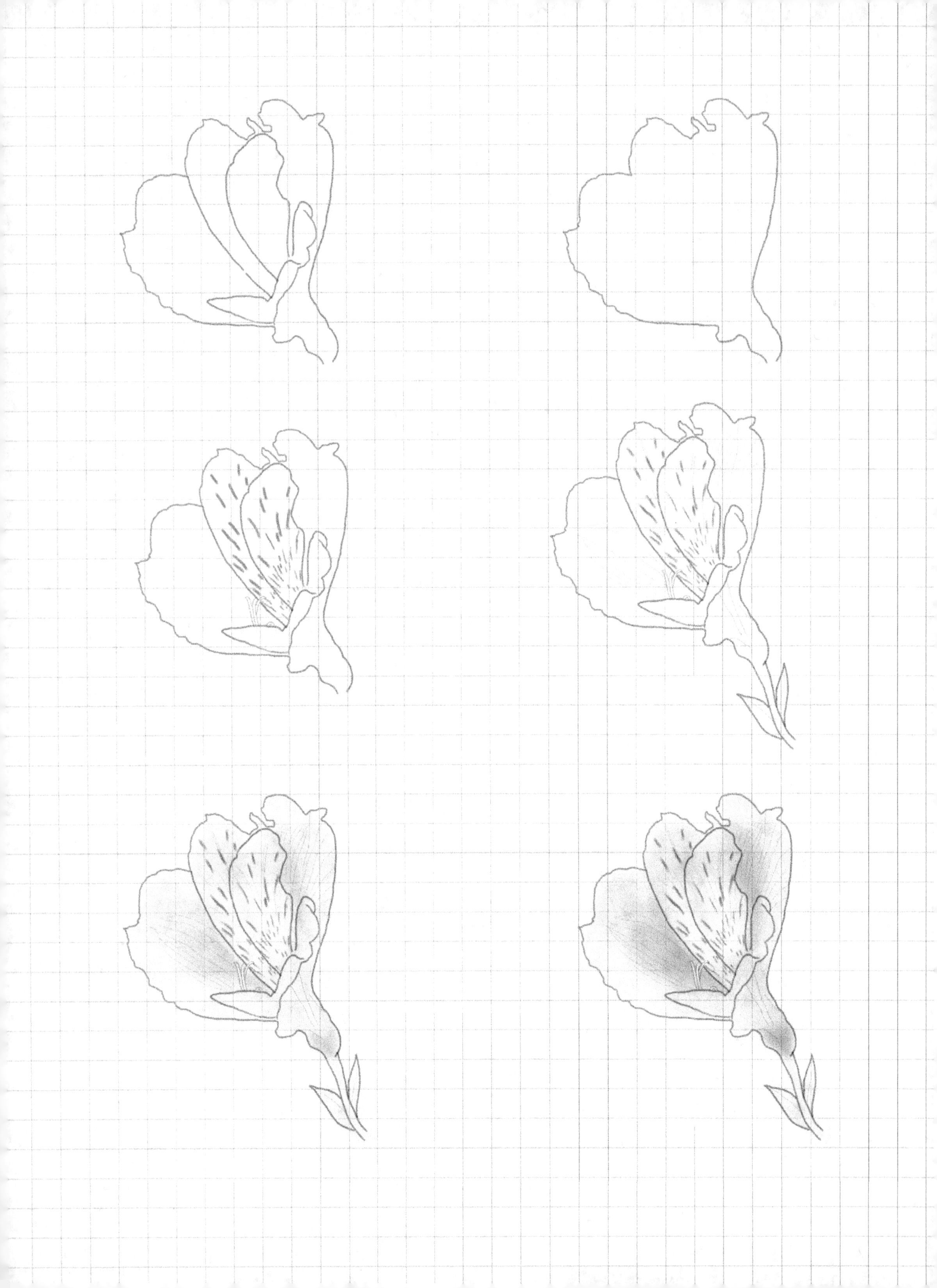

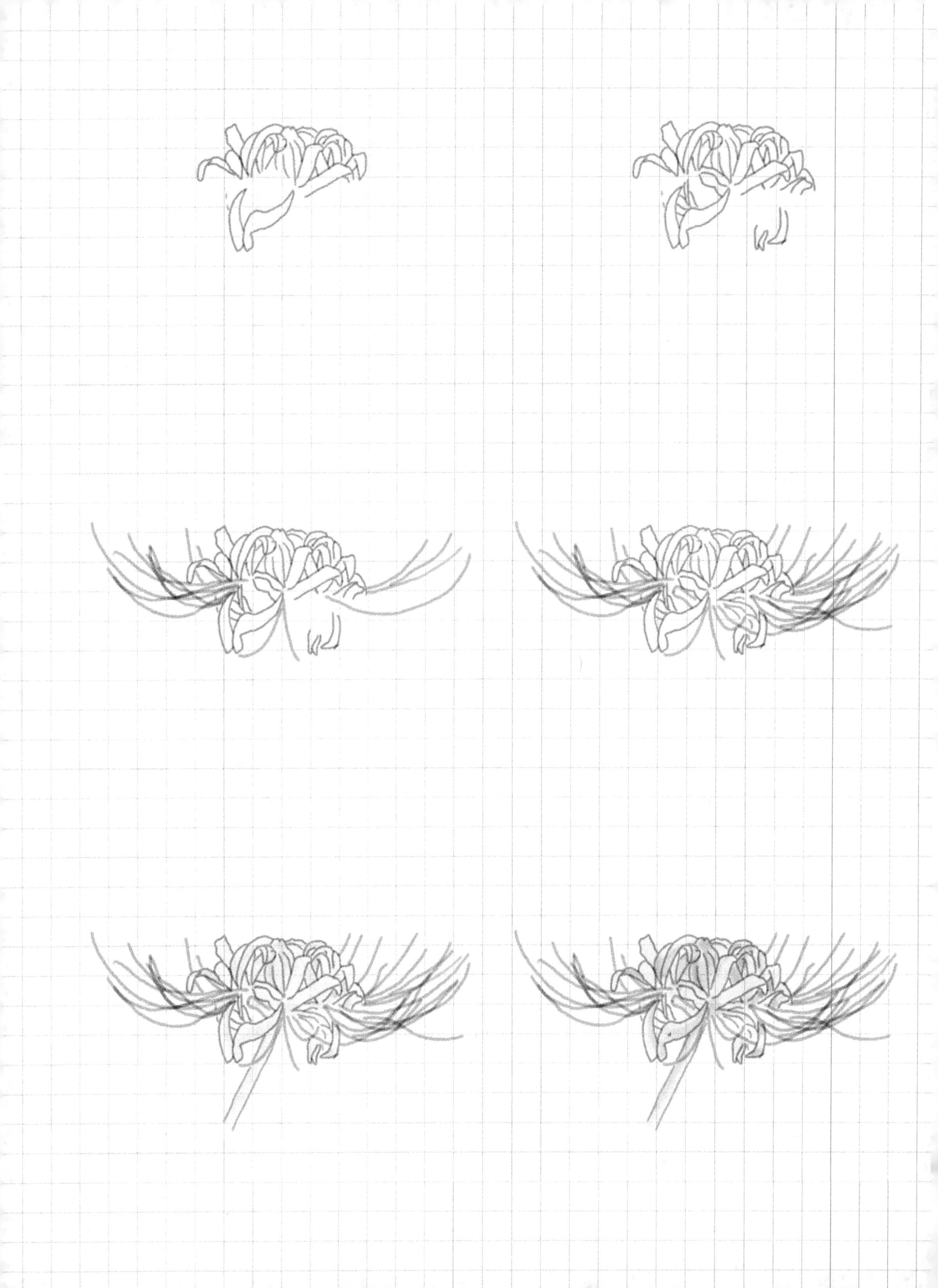

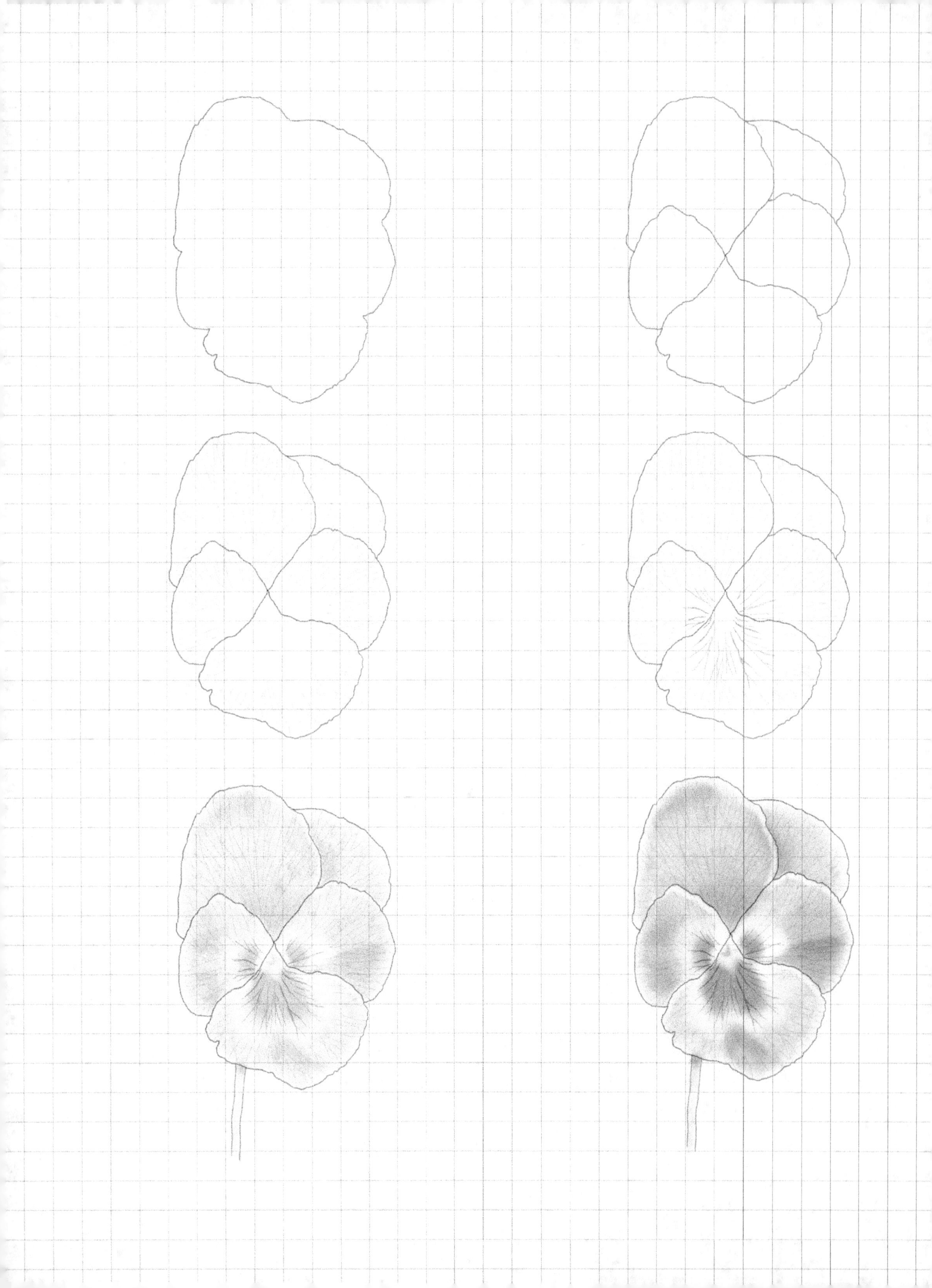

THANK YOU FOR YOUR PURCHASE!

We greatly appreciate your support. Without you, none of this would be possible. **Please consider leaving us a review on Amazon.** Reviews greatly help us to be able to continue to produce books such as this one. Also, feel free to follow us on our social media channels or contact us directly at **sketchpert.press@gmail.com**

And be sure to join our exclusive Facebook Group for freebies, giveaways, and early preview copies!

@sketchperts

@sketchperts